How My Mother Met STALIN

EIGHTEEN VERY SHORT STORIES

BORKO JOVANOVIC

Front cover photo:
Author with his mother, in 1957 Kalemegdan Park, Belgrade

ISBN: 1463500645
ISBN-13: 9781463500641

Contents

PREFACE

Every immigrant carries a load of memories, as no one leaves his or her country of origin for no good reason. I wrote the stories that follow for myself, for my wife, for my mother, and for my friends. Some of the material was originally written for the Chicago-based bilingual *Journal of the Serbian Academic Club,* which no longer exists.

There is so much history in each person that there is no chance much of it can be told (Proust comes to mind). My preference is to pick up something that may carry a ten-minute "telling," write it down, and let the rest be inferred.

All of the stories in this book are about real events; some of the names I have changed, and some I have not. My interpretation of history is that of an ordinary person who had to live it or had to hear about it. Therefore, I do not claim precision in this department, but I do claim a decent approximation of it.

My mother, Branka, was born in 1921 in Sarajevo, the second child of three and the only daughter of an officer in the pre-World War II Yugoslavian Army. My grandfather Stevan Zivkovic served in the Serbian Army in World War I, fought the Austrians in Serbia in 1914 and 1915, and crossed Albania on foot as the Serbian Army retreated to Greece. In 1917, the Serbian Army returned and rejuvenated by the help of the French and the British in Greece, won the war in the Balkans and liberated Serbia. That was the end of the Austro-Hungarian Empire, as well as the end of the Ottoman Empire. A new country called Yugoslavia was born.

My grandfather then became an officer in the newly formed Yugoslav Army, where he rose to the rank of colonel and served in Dubrovnik, Sarajevo, and Prizren (in the present Former Yugoslav Republic of Macedonia). He retired to Belgrade in 1939 with a good pension. His three children were aiming high: the eldest son, Brano, went to the Air Force Academy; my mother, Branka, studied French and Italian literature and fine arts; and the youngest son, Borko, planned to study law. Then, in 1941, World War II came along, and everything fell apart. The youngest son was eventually executed by the Communists, the eldest son was captured and imprisoned by the Germans, and my mother had to give up her studies and plans to visit France.

My grandfather Stevan, grandmother Jelena, and mother Branka survived the German bombing of

Belgrade in 1941, the American and British bombing in 1944 and 1945, and the Russian and Communist liberation of Belgrade in 1945. They got by in
part by selling off their furniture, art, and books. My
grandfather got a job as a construction supervisor.
In the liberation process, he had lost his pension,
though he later regained some of it. His two sons
were forever gone; the eldest surfaced many years
later in New York and Chicago; the youngest, who
had been shot by Tito's special troops, was thrown
into a pit at Kocevski Rog, Slovenia, with thousands
of other non-communist combatants. In the 1990s,
in Milwaukee, Wisconsin, I met a man (Mr. Ojdrovic)
who escaped this slaughter. He walked naked (according to him, they were all stripped of their
clothes and shot naked) for five days and got to Austria and eventually to the United States. He told me
that from his group about fifty of the men escaped.
He also told me that in the past he had contacted my
mother and informed her of what had happened to
her younger brother, Borko. She kept this secret to
herself, and their mother still hoped her youngest
child was alive at her own death in 1980.

After her marriage to my father, Dusan Jovanovic,
fell apart, my mother left her teaching job and
worked in Belgrade banks for the next thirty years.
She became an expert on foreign bank correspon-
dence, with French banks in particular. Since she
was not a member of the Communist Party, she was
only minimally promoted, but since she was good at

what she was doing and had a small child (myself), she was tolerated and used as needed.

She lived until I was fifty-five years old, reaching the good old age of eighty-seven. In all those years, I only heard her complain once, perhaps in the 1960s. When I asked her why she did not remarry, she said, "Alas, there are no good men left anywhere around here; there are only half-men walking the streets." I never asked again.

Thank you for your patience with the words that follow. They contain a bit of personal history, and I sincerely hope you will not think time spent reading them, was time wasted.

And to quote from the Steely Dan song: "Sue me if I play too long." [1]

---

[1] : Steely Dan: "Deacon Blues" from the album "Aja" (MCA Records, 1977).

1
How My Mother Met Stalin

The year was 1951 or 1952, and I had not been born yet. My parents lived and taught school in Vrsac, a town in northeast Yugoslavia, close to the Romanian border. After the 1948 breakaway from the Soviet Union, the Yugoslav Communist Party was divided; there were the pro-independence-minded, led by Tito, and the "Stalinists"—a general term for those more seriously devoted to the Soviet style of doing business.

To make a long story short, Stalinists were purged from the mainstream of society and the army. Many ended up on Goli Otok (Naked Island), a Yugoslav gulag, where one of the activities was carving Tito's name into a mountain. Consequently, many of those who subscribed to the old-fashioned Communism of the time and feared persecution for such beliefs escaped, or tried to escape, eastward, across one of the borders of the Soviet bloc countries: Hungary, Romania, and Bulgaria. For people living in Vrsac at

1

that time, because of their proximity to the Romanian border, a consequence of all this was that the army garrison in the vicinity of the town was large, so soldiers were a common sight in the streets. Many of the soldiers walked around with their dogs, well-trained military dogs, whose purpose was to track down and catch individuals trying to illegally cross the border.

The story begins one morning when my mother went into a bakery to buy bread. A huge German shepherd was sitting in the shop, staring at her. She made small talk with the soldier who handled the dog, and he assured her she could safely go about her business. And she did. On the way out, she followed the two and at some point got the idea that she wanted to pet the dog. "Pardon me," she said, perhaps slightly out of breath from catching up with them, "do you mind telling me about your dog? He is so good-looking and seems so well trained."

The soldier was kind. They stopped, and he explained to my mother that his dog was well trained indeed and, except for not being able to speak, was a "proper soldier all the way." The two lived together, sharing everything; they were practically like brothers. In particular, the dog was well behaved on public transportation and never spilled water or food when he was fed. His job was to locate the unfortunate person trying to cross the border, knock him down to the ground, and lie on top of him until the rest of the crew arrived to arrest him. "He would never hurt anyone unless ordered to do so," the soldier assured my mother.

After exchanging a few more words with the soldier, my mother asked if she could pet the animal.

"You may shake his paw if you wish," the soldier replied.

Perhaps slightly disappointed but not willing to argue, she agreed.

The soldier then turned to the dog, who was sitting properly by his side, and said, "Stalin, shake comrade's hand." Stalin dutifully raised his paw.

My mother was stunned. "His name is Stalin?"

"Yes, comrade," the soldier patiently replied. "We also have Molotov and Beria in our unit."

And so my mother, in 1951 or 1952, on a street in Vrsac, met Stalin, although she had never had the good fortune to meet either Molotov or Beria.

For better or for worse, the rest is history.

2
To Be with the People

The year AD 2005 had it that May 1, a great international Communist holiday (incidentally, set in memory of the 1886 Haymarket Massacre of workers in Chicago) and Serbian Orthodox Easter fell on the same day. For people who grew up in the former Yugoslavia, this is another tongue-in-cheek reminder of how complicated and possibly absurd things can get.

For my mother, I know, days like this brought back interesting memories, and needless to say, some of us had to hear them more than once. Here is one, and I am recording it not because I have nothing better to do, staring at the dunes of Lake Michigan on a cold weekend out of town, but because I have heard it so many times that on a day like this, I want it to be finally and officially recorded and put away.

In the provincial town of Vrsac, in post-World War II Yugoslavia, my mother taught Serbian and French literature at the local gymnasium. The year was approximately 1950. Now, although at that time, the expression of religious customs and sentiments was not banned by law, schoolteachers and "educators" in general were expected *not* to attend religious services, lest they influence, even in subtle ways, the young generation, the future of Socialist Yugoslavia.

My mother did not really go to church much, but thought it appropriate (and safe in both directions) to attend a church service once in a while, shall we say on Christmas Eve and on Easter. She thus defied the expectations of the state in control but also underperformed in regular Sunday service attendance of the Church Services Department. So, on an Easter Sunday, circa 1950, my mother dressed up nicely, kissed her husband good-bye (my father preferred to mark religious holidays with a visit to a local tavern—a very safe choice at the time), and walked slowly down Main Street to the Serbian Orthodox Church.

Sitting on a bench across the street and reading a newspaper was the gymnasium principal, Comrade Kovac. My mother was happy he did not seem to notice her, as he was apparently deeply involved with latest news about the deepening divide between the Yugoslav and the Soviet Communist Parties. In the church, the Easter service went well, and my mother returned home happily.

The next day, at school, she was invited to visit the principal in his office. "Comrade Jovanovic," Comrade Kovac said to her with gravitas in his voice, "you were seen entering an Orthodox Church yesterday. I have no words to express my disgust and disappointment! You, an educator of new generations!"

The thing was settled after my father (who taught philosophy and sociology at the same school) threatened Comrade Kovac with bodily harm (my mother was pregnant at the time) and she promised to give a lecture entitled "Religion—the Opium of the Masses."

Some fifty years later, my mother attended an Easter service in the newly built Orthodox cathedral in Belgrade. As the congregation sang the hymns, she noticed the presence of a beautiful male voice in her vicinity.

Slowly turning to investigate whom the voice belonged to, she, to her disdain, saw that the voice belonged to Comrade Kovac. He was standing there, much older of course, but he was singing along, and quite a voice he had! More than fifty years had gone by, but my mother would not let this pass so easily.

She slowly moved in his direction until their elbows touched. "What are you doing here, singing in the church, Comrade Kovac?" she asked innocently.

"Ah, I am just trying to be with the people, as always," was his no-less-innocent answer.

And so they sang Easter hymns in unison, elbows touching—at least for a while.

3
How Great-Grandfather
Mika Died

Much has been written and said about Argentinean writer Jorge Luis Borges (1899–1986). Like many of my peers, I was taken by his prose in my younger years and still have most of his published works in my library. One of Borges's literary specialties was stories about people on the rough edge of life: summer heat, knives, assassins, honor, village dust caked by blood, and the local politics of nineteenth-century Argentina. I never felt that I could write down anything remotely as moving or as interesting, because I lacked talent and had no appropriate material. Recently, it occurred to me that the story of how Deda Mika died just might qualify, so talent aside, here it is.

About fifteen years ago, during one of my annual summer visits to the old country, I took two friends back to the village of my ancestors. The plan was somewhat prompted by convenience: my aunt Lala was spending a few weeks there "at the old house," and I needed a ride to see her and to inspect the ever-present damage to the property. My buddy Zvonko offered to give me a ride in his old but unbeatable Golf Volkswagen and a lady friend I acquired during the visit, Mila, had nothing better to do for the day, so the three of us took off for an hour and a half drive down the Beograd-Nis *Auto Put.* Needless to say, we had fun, although my two friends were a bit apprehensive, entering an unknown realm (Mila's folks had been city dwellers for a few generations, and Zvonko's family came from Croatia). The old Golf had a pretty good stereo system, and we put on some Led Zeppelin while enjoying the sights of the Serbian heartland.

Once we got off the highway, we easily found our way to the house I remembered from my childhood summer visits. It was just in town, across from the church and the only bridge in the village. We drove up to the property with great difficulty, because of the overgrown grass. My aunt greeted us and pulled out some food she had prepared. All was well in spite of the tremendous overgrowth of trees and vegetation, which showed the reality: no one lived there anymore.

As we were sinking into a mild stupor delivered by one single half-liter bottle of beer in the mid-July heat, my aunt began to tell us how her great-grandfather Mika (Deda Mika) was killed. I've no idea what prompted this, especially in light of the fact that we had just arrived. Possibly, she felt the need to tune my companions and myself (big city slickers) into the local scene, for I had heard this story before and more than once. I mention this because she did not even bother to ask my friends who they were and what they did with their lives. She just began to speak, as if driven by a demon.

In the late 1800s, Deda Mika was sitting one fine morning in front of the local café (*kafana*), which he owned, all dressed up, as always, in his dark, three-piece suit, when two scoundrels suddenly appeared. Now Deda Mika was of the "Radical" political persuasion, meaning he belonged to the Serbian Radical Party. The two scoundrels had been paid by the other party in power (here details grow scarce). They just walked up behind him, and one of them slit his throat. Then they ran away on foot.

Deda Mika sat there for a long time, pressing his white handkerchief to the wound, while everyone else was in great commotion. In the end, Deda Mika bled to death, and the handkerchief stained with his blood was passed down in the family. Presently, we do not know where it is, but it is possible it was thrown out during World War II, lest various warring fractions that came and went through the village thought this to be a sign of allegiance to the other side.

The perpetrators were caught within hours when their escape failed to realize. They were brought back to the village in chains. Deda Mika's two sons, both serving in an elite cavalry unit, were on the scene within two days. Court was assembled, and the assassins confessed to their crime. The sons made a request: they wanted to personally execute the criminals. This request was denied. The law must be obeyed, and it does not provide for personal vengeance. So the execution was carried out by the relevant powers, with his two sons present but not involved in the shooting. And people talked about the white handkerchief pressed upon Deda Mika's bleeding throat for a few generations.

After she finished the monologue, Aunt Lala snapped out of her trance and asked us if we were still hungry. We said, very politely, that we'd had enough, thank you. Then I got busy examining the property and taking note of various damage caused by the elements and uncaring neighbors. As the July sun was setting, the three of us agreed it was time to return to Belgrade.

On the way back, we were silent. There was not much to say. I felt sorry for my companions. I thought we should listen to Led Zeppelin some more, but somehow, it did not feel right. When we reached Belgrade, the city lights were coming on.

As we parted ways, I thanked my companions for spending the day with me and said something like, "Onward into the future," in a voice that was not quite mine. They both nodded at the same time, as if all was well and understood.

I went home and poured myself a large glass of brandy. As my native village persona dissolved and my literary ego kicked in, I thought of Jorge Louis Borges.

I knew that I would have to write Lala's story down, one fine day. It only took me fifteen years.

4
Bread and Chocolate

Recently, my wife, Lisa, and I discovered Vosges chocolate bars. The label reads, "*Haut Chocolat,*" which, translated from the French into plain English, means "fancy chocolate." The initial interest was, of course, purely scientific: we wanted to taste the stuff. It was very good. It saved a lot of money to have the stuff handy and skip a trip to France. We were very pleased with the Naga Bar (Indian curry, coconut flakes, and milk) and especially with the Red Fire Bar (Mexican ancho y chipotle, chili peppers, Ceylon cinnamon, and dark chocolate).

"Yummm," said my wife, in a fairly scientific tone. I remained objectively silent.

One night, feeling a bit on the wild side, I pulled out a Red Fire Bar and announced to my wife, "We will be having French bread with French *chocolat*!"

She was pleased. "Wow, how interesting—how did you come up with that idea?"

"My mother taught me," I said after giving it some thought.

And then it all came back to me. When I was a boy, *Zvecevo* chocolates were the thing. I remember when they first came out circa 1960, with the big (half kilo?) package, containing about ten bars one could break off. It was serious business; we got one for New Year and maybe one for school graduation. Now this is how I learned about bread and chocolate.

At that time, my mother was working at the National Bank in Belgrade, and it so happened they had a New Year's Day celebration; this was perhaps around 1965. A big *Zvecevo* chocolate package was brought out, and each person got a bar. Mr. Savich, one of the supervisors, took his bar and began to walk away. Mr. Savich was not particularly well liked. He was a mousy, gray, half-bald, and short guy—a meticulous pain in the neck. He imperiously ran the French department, which consisted of twenty women.

"Where are you going, Mr. Savich?" asked my mother, perhaps not entirely innocently.

"To my office, comrade," replied he.

"But why?" my mother asked.

"Because, Madame Zivkovic," Mr. Savich replied (in French, as it was the French department), "in my desk drawer, I have a piece of bread, and I will eat my chocolate with my piece of bread."

"How interesting," my mother opined, again perhaps not entirely innocently.

"Yes, *madame*," he replied. "In France, this is normal. My mother was French, as you know. We always ate our chocolate with bread. It tastes better. Besides, this will provide a lunch for me costing only two dinars, which is exactly what I paid for a slice of bread in the canteen."

"How clever of you," my mother said, "but you are depriving us of your good company."

Without further comment, Mr. Savich quickly disappeared into his office, clutching his chocolate bar.

In a different setting, as I write this, I see a photograph of my grandfather, Stevan Zivkovic, taken in 1915. He is among a group of fellow officers at exercise at Mali Pozarevac, srez Grocanski, just as World War I was beginning. For some reason, shortly after the above-described chocolate event, my mother showed this photo to Mr. Savich, who recognized one of the high-ranking officers sitting in the center as his own father.

Perhaps to get even with her, he said to my mother, "Is it not funny, Madame Zivkovic, that my father commanded your father, and here I command you?"

"Yes, indeed," she replied. "I only wonder if he too ate his provisions alone."

And so, many years later, following this dusty trail of cocoa all the way to Chicago, the story came alive for us. I am not sure what it all means, but now I cannot separate it from the taste of bread and chocolate in my mouth, a taste that still gives me enormous pleasure.

5
In Ancient Greece

The following message came down to me via the Internet, sent by, of all people, my mother-in-law, Joyce.

In ancient Greece, Socrates (469–399 BC) was widely lauded for his wisdom. One day, the great philosopher spotted an acquaintance, who ran up to him excitedly and said, "Socrates, do you know what I just heard about one of your students?"

"Wait a moment," Socrates replied. "Before you tell me, I'd like you to pass a little test. It's called the Test of Three."

"Three?"

"That's right," Socrates continued. "Before you talk to me about my student, let's take a moment to test what you're going to say.

"The first test is truth. Have you made absolutely sure that what you are about to tell me is true?"

"No," the man said, "actually, I just heard about it."

"All right," said Socrates, "so you don't really know if it's true or not. Now let's try the second test, the test of goodness. Is what you are about to tell me about my student something good?"

"No, on the contrary…"

"So," Socrates continued, "you want to tell me something bad about him even though you're not certain it's true?"

The man shrugged, a little embarrassed.

Socrates continued, "You may still pass, though, because there is a third test—the filter of usefulness. Is what you want to tell me about my student going to be useful to me?"

"No, not really…"

"Well," concluded Socrates, "if what you want to tell me is neither true nor good nor even useful, why tell it to me at all?"

The man was defeated and ashamed. This is the reason Socrates was a great philosopher and held in such high esteem.

It also explains why he never found out that his student Plato was having an affair with his wife.

This perhaps only mildly amusing story brings to mind its Serbian counterpart, albeit from the Communist Era, but equally, as the English would say, "saucy."

Two good friends, Pera and Mika were discussing politics. At some point, irritated by his companion's ignorance, Pera asked Mika, "Okay, Mika, do you know who Karl Marx was?"

"Sounds very familiar, but I am not sure," said Mika.

"Fine, then do you know who Lenin was?" Pera continued.

"He was a Russian," replied Mika after some thought. "A big shot?"

"How about Trotsky?" was the third question.

Mika was not sure again.

"Well," said Pera, " you should, like me, take evening classes on Marxism, at the local Communist Party school, and you will know more about the world and about politics."

Mika was a bit miffed. "Okay," he said, "let me ask you something. Do you know who Laza is?"

"Laza? I have no idea," said Pera.

"Well, he is the guy who is having an affair with your wife while you take evening classes at the local Party school."

The message seems clear. We are all just reliving a version of the ancient past. Also, words of wisdom may actually trickle down the Internet, albeit altered by an accidental interpreter. I will try to remember all this.

In the meantime, I am quitting my Spanish evening class. It is a pity, for I was looking forward to studying *Don Quixote* and reading it aloud to my wife in the original seventeenth-century Spanish.

6
The Importance of Being a Von

My wife, Lisa, is a von (Drehle), as is her father, Ray; her sister Carin; her mother Joyce and the rest of their family. My brother-in-law, Paul, is a ver (Bruggen). In the local parlance around the Queen's Park area of London, they say that "von kicks ver's butt." This is just a small family joke, a propos the Germans and the Dutch, and an inside joke of Carin and Paul's.

Now I am a (Jovano) vic. Paul tells me it stands for "ordinary Joe" in Serbian. I like it, although my late aunt Milanka went to great pains to produce (without success) proof of our family's seminobility, dating from nineteenth-century Serbia. Semi (whatever it means) seems to be better than nothing. But, whatever we are, we are proud of it. The vons however, do seem to have a better chance of having had nobility in the past, and this seemed to us even more possible once we discovered a town in Germany by the name of Drehle.

Be that as it may, some years ago, as Lisa and I were making preparations for our wedding, we were introduced to a caterer by the name of Guido von Aulach. Quite a name, we thought, and the food he prepared was excellent. "Would it not be great to have nobility serve at our wedding?" we joked and went to meet Guido and his wife.

They lived in Des Plaines, Illinois, in a very small, very ordinary house and ran their business from home. They had eight young children, all of whom, they proudly told us, were homeschooled. We were impressed. At some point during the evening, Lisa mentioned that she too "is a von." We were hoping this would lead into a bit of an interesting conversation about history, if nothing else.

"Perhaps we are both nobility," she added somewhat too innocently, looking at Guido.

"Perhaps," he replied rather seriously, "and from what century do you think is your title?"

We were speechless for a moment. "Well, I have no idea," Lisa answered. "Fifteenth or sixteenth maybe?" The truth is we knew nothing about it.

Well," said Guido rather somberly, "the real vons come from the eleventh century, although there are a few from the seventeenth."

"Okay then, probably from the seventeenth," my wife-to-be answered quickly, to take a lesser position and thus settle the matter.

"Let me check," said Guido. "I just happen to have the right book handy." He rose from his rather old and battered circa 1950s armchair and walked over to an untidy bookshelf. He pulled out a medium-sized volume and said to us with a certain smile, "We are all listed here, with all descendants up to about five years ago. Let me see if your name appears under D."

He searched the pages in vain. "I am very sorry, but your family does not seem to be listed," he finally said with a sigh. "My family is listed under A," he added, "and we are from the eleventh century." He showed us the relevant pages. We took the time to examine the book. It contained a fairly detailed list of surnames and first names including those of wives, children, and the deceased. Von Aulach was listed on one of the first ten or twenty pages. He himself, his wife, and some of their children were properly enumerated. We were very impressed. After a bit of a pause, the conversation returned to the menu, and we agreed about all of the necessary details for the occasion.

The wedding went very well, I am happy to say, and the food prepared by Guido von Aulach was quite a success. Although some of the guests in attendance might have thought I was marrying into nobility, only very few knew that we were being served by the real eleventh-century vons.

Sooner or later, however, truth trickles out.

7
Lice Na Frot

A few years ago, our condominium association decided we needed a handyman for the building, for "small jobs"—garbage removal and such. I volunteered to locate and supervise such a person.

After some inquires, a man was recommended to us, someone who, as they said, was "from the old country." I met this man, and let us call him Meho. The name suggested he was from Bosnia, and this, given the recent war in the former republics of the former Yugoslavia, gave me a bit of pleasure in hiring him; it implied we were going to help him out in his new life in the New World, as much as he was going to help us.

He was a large man, in his fifties, and had little to say. He made it plain that he understood what the job entailed and that we should have no worries about it for he took care of another, much larger building. I spoke with him in a mixture of English and Serbian, trying not to pry into his exact origins and his former life. But as I said, our conversation was limited. We avoided references to national or linguistic denominations, and I think that was fine with both of us.

The following week, I posted his "work list" on the bulletin board in the lobby. It was in English, for I gathered this was the lingua franca of building managers in Chicago, and I did not want to suggest he had to speak Serbian. Meho was supposed to write in his hours and the tasks he performed on a weekly basis.

Several weeks went by, but nothing appeared on the list, although some jobs did seem to have been done—garbage removal in particular. I kept my eye out for possible evidence of staircase vacuuming, but the dust seemed to grow instead of disappear. I thought about this for a while and decided that he could not read English. So I wrote a note in Serbian, using the Cyrillic alphabet. A few more weeks went by with no result. I decided then that he could not read Cyrillic (or he was offended by it) and wrote the note in the Latin script. Nothing changed—the garbage was out, and some jobs were done, but the general state of affairs was not to our satisfaction.

Finally, I called his house, and his son picked up the phone. We spoke to each other in English, and I explained to him who I was and that Meho needed to write in his hours and tasks. The young man was very pleasant, and he spoke without foreign accent or fault. He promised his father would get the message.

Soon thereafter, a strange sequence of messages began to appear on the bulletin board. They seemed strange because I could not understand much and could not decipher what language they were written in. Here are some examples: "Pon. Stakla na lobu. Tue. Lice na frot. Petak. Dast lobu. Mop lobu. Novi balb."

At the same time, the dust on our staircase continued to accumulate, although I explicitly requested some serious vacuuming. It took me a while to understand what was going on.

Meho apparently could write only in a mix of two languages. Thus "lobu" = lobby, "dast" = dust, "balb" = lightbulb, and the rest was in…well, let us say in Serbian…at least some of the days of the week…who can tell?

"Lice na frot" was the most difficult to decipher. My wife took on the task, and after a few more weeks, she mentioned that Meho was very keen on using the leaf blower (his own equipment) in the front of the building, blowing, as she put it, "the hell out of our grass." So after some thought we understood: "*lice na frot*" = lisce (leaves); (na = in front of the); frot = front (front of the entrance door).

I think this was his favorite task, as he used to perform it diligently early on Saturday mornings.

As for never using the vacuum cleaner, I decided I would let that pass. Perhaps he had something against vacuum cleaners. We waited for the Christmas season to come and go, and shortly thereafter, I wrote Meho a check and a note thanking him for the work he had done and letting him know that we would take care of the building ourselves and hire professional cleaners for the lobby and staircase. Meho promptly left the keys at the bulletin board, and that was that.

Looking back, I think we know only part of the story. I'd say that Meho came over from the old country a long time ago (and not recently, following the civil war, as we had thought) and that he had been illiterate at the time. He picked up enough English to get by, but clearly never learned to read or write properly in either language. He was fine with using his own noisy leaf blower every Saturday morning to our chagrin, but vacuuming the hallway was not something he would do, although he would not admit it. Perhaps this was beyond his technical prowess or contrary to his honor or beliefs. I'll never know.

Although we probably royally overpaid him for blowing the leaves in front of the building and taking the garbage out, we still think of him fondly.

Each fall, once a week or so, facing a heap of leaves in front of our doorway, my wife and I look at each other and say in unison, with some strange sense of nostalgia, "Lice na frot!"

8
My Wife and Tosha the Cat

For some time now, I have been waiting for signs of my wife's, hopefully mild, attraction to… another someone. We have been happily married for a few years, and lately, while browsing through newspapers and magazines together, we have allowed ourselves the liberty of noting that this or that famous person or fashion model "looks cute." In this domain, I should mention that my interest in a certain Land's End summer catalogue was in part prompted by the fact that one of the swimsuit models was *really* cute.

My wife said it was okay if I kept my eye on the woman "for a couple of days." This was fine with me, and I am happy to report this was just a brief summer thing.

And for my wife's part, during our recent trip to Montenegro, we encountered someone she was really moved by. We stayed for a week at the Palas Hotel in Petrovac, and following a major advertising effort by a traveling theater troupe from Subotica, one evening, we attended a play. The play, by Branko Copic, was entitled, *Dozivljaji Macka Toshe* (*Adventures of Tosha the Cat*).

This is a children's play, and adults were admitted free of charge. All actors were in large animal costumes, most notably Tosha the Cat and a couple of oversized mice.

In brief, the story is that Tosha is a lazy country cat who does not do a great job of keeping mice away from his master's barn. The master is angry and makes plans to get rid of Tosha. All ends well, with Tosha promising to be more alert in the barn and less in the bacon department. He is of course quite lovable and sings many songs, which, I suppose, make this play a bit of a Serbian countryside *operetta.*

The main song goes something like this.

> *Tooosho, Tooosho, bubo leeenja*
> *Stooo se teeebi uvek dreeema…*
> (Tosha, Tosha, you lazy cat
> always looking for a place to nap…)

All the two hundred or so children in the audience sang along, and we, the adults, sang along too.

Later that evening, my wife said, "That Tosha, he is really cute."

My ears perked up. I said nothing. Then, when we went to bed, she sang in Serbian: "*Tooosho, Tooosho, bubo leeenja…*" In the weeks that followed, I overheard her mumble Tosha's name in the shower, in the car, at her desk: "Tosho, Tosho, you lazy cat, always looking for a place to nap…" A bit strange, to say the least. Seemed like a true attraction.

I suppose I will just have to live with Tosha for a while. Our two cats, having never caught a mouse in a barn, keep their silence as well. That's married life.

At least I know Tosha is still probably in Montenegro, where for all I care, he can stay.

9
Daddy

Daddy is the best in everything. Daddy's opinion is important. He thinks *great thoughts*. He shares them, sometimes. Such moments are great moments, moments of the wisdom of Daddy. Daddy has an audience of one: his wife, Mrs. Daddy. None else knows Daddy exists. Only Mrs. Daddy and Daddy know Daddy exists.

The idea of Daddy is greater than Daddy. That is the only thing greater than Him. Daddy is in everything. Daddy is an archetype. In fact, He is the most important archetype. Daddy. Daddy. Daddy.

My half-brother Mike is a major talker. He is properly married and has a proper job. He is a professor of sociolinguistics. He never shuts up. His views are many and continuous. His wife and their son always only listen; they are used to it. The last time I saw him, I said, "Don't you have anything to ask me?"

"What could I ask you?" he replied.

I am the president in *Moon over Parador,* Richard Dreyfus in the role, but I do take over. I address my citizens: "You are my *broders.* You are my *seesters.* You are my *neeeces* and nephews…and for that matter, many of you are my *cheeeldren.* You are the *reeson* I am here, your *presidente.* I *leeve forr* you. And I promise to you that I will *faaaaight* for the *honur* and for the *leeeberty* of Parador to the last drop of my *blud*" (Ovations).

Daddy takes the stage. He is the best actor. He plays Daddy. He strikes a pose, something like Mussolini on stage—his fists in his sides, elbows out, chest puffed up, head slightly turned to the side. "Daddy is important," he says.

Mrs. Daddy says, "Yeees."

Stalin had a great moustache. When he stayed up at night, all government offices in Moscow stayed up, just in case He called. And he stayed up late a lot.

Daddy's opinion is important. He told his wife last week that "the war will start on Saturday." He was wrong. But she did understand; Daddy's opinion is important. And he cares. "I am glad they did not listen to you this time," she said.

Daddy is incredibly strong. This is a given. Mrs. Daddy always reminds him of how strong he is. He always opens jars for her, at the kitchen counter, because he is the strongest—jars of *pindjur* from Macedonia and *ajvar* from Croatia.

Daddy has seen it all. His judgments are brief: "Been there, done that," he says. Mrs. Daddy is glad this is the case as far as other ladies are concerned.

"No need to snoop around," Daddy says. "I've done it—lots of crazy stuff. Not worth the bother."

Mrs. Daddy smiles.

Daddy is a weapons expert. He used an AK-47 in the army. And the big machine gun. "That thing will cut up a tree," he says. "With pistol," he says, "I was the second best in the company. One Albanian was better, but we were close."

Mrs. Daddy nods in approval. "I can't believe you were not the best," she says.

"I never threw a hand grenade," Daddy says, trying to be completely truthful about it. "It was optional."

Luba's father was on Goli Otok, "The Naked Island," a notorious political prisoners' camp. He swore at Tito, in public, in 1950. He came back as an old man, eight years later. I sort of remember him, sitting in their garden, in our Belgrade neighborhood, a quiet, tough, very old man with a white moustache. He mainly read the newspapers and smiled at us.

My father liked to take me for a walk downtown on Sundays. We'd go from one bar to the next. He showed me to his friends. "My first pedagogical production," he would proudly say. They smiled and raised their glasses to my health. I'd drink raspberry juice and get really bored. All the action was above the counter, and I was too short to see it. I'd watch their shoes and what they pulled out of their pockets. And ladies' legs too. Daddy action.

"To be continued" is an understatement. The Daddy Chronicles never end. Daddy is 4-ever.

10
I Do Have Friends

I am quite surprised by this news. My fiftieth birthday approaching, I realized that I had stopped calling my old girlfriends and my former wife at least five years ago. Rob married Marj, and they live in New Hampshire now. William and Martha have moved to New York. Peter is in town but lives in an ashram, and he does not drink anymore. Nebe and Misha have faded away in their parallel but separate reality in Belgrade. Tom is in Paris, cooking away for Marie-Claude and reading the *Wall Street Journal*. Adrian has stopped calling, since he and Nina broke up.

My mother, Branka, who is staying with us for the winter, brought the issue to me rather abruptly. My wife, Lisa, was away on business, for a week, and after four or five evenings loaded with silence, while I was at my usual place by the computer, my mother spoke. She asked, "Do you not have any friends anymore?"

Truth be told, none had called, and I called none. I know my mother was keeping an eye on me—for security reasons: she is very fond of my second wife, Lisa, and hopes we stay together forever. I hope so too. I am quite happy staying up alone at night when Lisa is away. And I stay up pretty late when she is around as well—although not as late, as she has a special way of telling me I should come to bed real soon.

Be that as it may, it took me a while to respond to my mother's question. "Hmmm," I said, "all my friends are out of town. Besides, it is another winter in Chicago, and who wants to go out?" But the question remained, and I dwelled upon it for some time. Basically, like most people, I like to think I do have friends I can call up to chitchat or to discuss important matters with.

It was almost embarrassing to admit that perhaps I do not have such friends anymore!

The very next day, as I was checking my e-mail, I realized that there are people out there who may be my friends. I am speaking of Richard Jouel, Dr. Thomas Fawundu, Chief Topa Ibe, Mr. Robert Mark, Mr. Calson Alewa, Dr. Olu Jacobs, and Mr. Edwin Carley, to name but a few. The strange thing is, they all seem to be from Africa, and I wonder whether they know each other. The matter is a bit, shall we say, dicey. But their words seem true, and there seems to be a possible financial gain in this.

Before I get into details, let me just proudly say that my personal qualities have been recognized by these gentlemen through the virtue of the Internet. I do have a Web site, and my accomplishments are all clearly listed if you Google my name.

But I digress. Here is what Richard Jouel has to say:

I am Richard Jouel, the Auditor General of a bank in Africa, during the course of our auditing I discovered a floating fund in an account opened in the bank in 1990 and since 1993 nobody has operated on this account again, after going through some old files in the records I discovered that the owner of the account died without a [heir] hence the money is floating and if I do not remit this money out urgently it will be forfeited for nothing. We will start the first transfer with Twenty six million [$26,000.000] upon successful transaction without any disappoint from your side, we shall re-apply for the payment of the remaining rest amount to your account.

Dr Thomas Fawundu had a similar story to tell:

Dear sir, It is my honour and confidence to introduce you to this business in view of the fact that you will be trustworthy and reliable and also beleiving in God that you shall not let me down, concerning this business. I am Dr. Thomas Fawundu, the Auditor General of the United Bank for Africa (UBA). During the course of our auditing in our Enugu State Branch in Nigeria, i discovered a floating fund in an account opened in the bank in 1990 and since 1993 nobody has operated on this account…

These gentlemen seem trustworthy, and Chief Topa Ibe confirms the gist of the story:

> *I have therefore been mandated as a matter of trust by my partners to source for a business partner to whom we could transfer the sum of USD33.2M by drawing up a letter of domiciliation instructing the concerned government to pay into the partner's account the contractual entitlement of USD33.2M.*

In fact, I have a visitor to look forward to:

> *I will apply for annual leave to get visa immediately, if i hear from you that you are ready to act and receive this fund in your account. I will use my position and influence to obtain all legal approvals for onward transfer of this money to your account with appropriate clearance from the relevant ministries and foreign exchange departments. Yours truly, Dr. Thomas Fawundu*

Sounds like a good deal. I did wonder how these gentlemen understood I am a trustworthy person. How did they find me, in my solitary, late-night-oriented existence? Here's the answer: *"I got your contact address from the Girl who operates computer"* (Mr. Calson).

The bottom line is this: I do have friends. They may not be 100 percent legitimate, but they mean well, and they trust me. My mother and my wife will be happy when they find out how much money I've made, sitting at home alone. With this kind of money, more friends will come forward. I shall buy a box of chocolates for that Girl Who Operates the Computer! And I remain virtually yours, especially if you have as good an understanding of my good qualities as some people seem to.

After a man reaches certain age, true friends are hard to find, but I am still available, though most likely not for very long.

11
The American Contractor

If you live in Chicago, you know that most building and remodeling jobs are done by Eastern Europeans— Poles, Serbs, Bosnians, Romanians, Macedonians, you can take your pick. If you are of a certain ethnic heritage, you may choose a contractor who may be your "*lantzman*" or "*zemljak*," that is, your "homeboy." This may or may not be a good idea.

Some time ago, my wife, Lisa, and I decided to renovate our kitchen. We promptly hired a contractor, "an American," as the rumor had it that "others" (read: Eastern Europeans) took too much time to do the job and were not entirely reliable. Things went well in April when they basically destroyed what we used to know as our kitchen. Our contractor, Mark Tudor, was a very nice man in his forties. He responded promptly to my wife's telephone calls (this was one of the reasons we hired him) and managed several crews, who showed professionalism and respect to our home and to us. It was all fine and dandy as we took measurements for the cabinets, which were to be custom made to my wife's and our architect's strict demands. The due date was set to be around July 4, when we were going to have a guest stay with us. Sometime in June, it became apparent that things were a bit delayed, and we settled on the fact that it would take "a few more weeks" to do the job. Our guest, Matt Swan, my wife's godson, a fine young man from Cambridge, England, survived the pizza meals and dry sausage snacks; it helped that he was in his teens and from England, and thus, at least in principle, used to…well, lesser food.

I was too busy working and writing a presentation for an early August conference to pay attention to kitchen renovation, but sometime in mid-August, facing an empty and desolate space in the midst of our home, we realized that something was not quite right. As Lisa was managing the entire undertaking, I gently inquired whether she thought that I should get involved. After some thought, she agreed that I should.

I made the call. "Mark," I said, "I am making this one call, and I hope you will get my message. The message is this: if you want to get paid, you have to deliver." Mark took it in and then called my wife three times that day. The thing was that the cabinet-maker, who was Romanian, was late with his work. I was pleased that Mark was serious about what we expected of him and that our decision not to hire Eastern Europeans proved to be correct. Here is one on the team, and he is making us all wait!

During the following week, things began to happen. It took another month and a half for the kitchen to be in reasonable shape, cabinets and all. After all was said and done, Mark agreed to paint our living room and the hallway free of charge. We were pleased. So on a nice autumn morning, in our new kitchen, I said to Mark, "We chose you because you are an American. And still you took so long! I guess it is because of the Romanian cabinetmaker!"

To this, Mark replied, "Well, actually, I am Macedonian, although I was born in Birmingham, Michigan. My parents changed their name from Todorovski to Tudor. And I will not take your remark personally!" I was grateful for his generosity and understanding in this delicate ethnic matter.

This morning, as I was making my first cup of coffee in our new kitchen, I realized that I did not know where the coffee beans came from. It may not seem an important matter, at 7:00 a.m., but I did wonder, for a moment. Possibly they came from Brazil or Colombia or Equador, but it may be difficult to tell.

Perhaps I will just have to settle for what it says on the label: "Organically grown and carefully selected for your long-lasting enjoyment."

12
Mr. Kubikas

I've known for some time that I married a strong woman when I married Lisa. However, the other day, the issue came up in an unexpected way. What happened was Lisa carried upstairs to our third-floor apartment the new plastic Christmas tree that she had just bought, all packed up in a box and made in China. I was away at work, and my mother, Branka, who was staying with us for the holidays, gave my wife the ultimate compliment, "You are so strong."

"Yes," my wife replied, "I am, after all, Mrs. Kubi-kas." A next-door neighbor overheard this conversation and wondered if perhaps Kubikas was our real (and secret, from a past unbecoming life) last name. The truth is, however, as follows.

I was born in the provincial town of Vrsac, in the former Yugoslavia. My mother lost her first child because of a hospital official's negligence and decided to stay at home for the birth of her second child, namely me. A woman was promptly chosen to assist her. She was Hungarian, and her name was Luca Neni.

When I was about to come out, Luca Neni was called in, and she was there in time for the event. When I came out, as my mother tells it, she picked me up by my legs, slapped me across my bottom and declared in broken Serbian, with a Hungarian accent: "*No, ti budes kubikas*," which, roughly translated, means, "Well, you are going to be a physical laborer," implying that I would be "a very strong man." *Kubik* is a measure of volume, precisely one meter cubed, which weighs a ton, if it contains water, to be scientific about it.

Kubikas is then basically a strong man who shovels cement, I think.

My mother tells this story at the drop of a hat, and needless to say, we deal with it the best we can. Slowly, it became a staple in our vocabulary, and my wife uses it whenever I am called on to carry something like the groceries upstairs. "Mr. Kubikas," she says, "there are a few things for you down at the bottom of the stairs."

Now I hate to carry stuff upstairs and often let out a donkey call when I am done. That is to say, I let everyone know how much I suffered in the process. (Please do not blog this information.)

A real kubikas would be proud of showing a bit of muscle action and perseverance, but alas, I am not one. So, Luca Neni was wrong, and although I am reasonably strong for my age, I am not anything like a kubikas. I do shovel snow in winter, but as little as I can get away with. However, if the essence is not there, the name "Kubikas" still remains attached to my persona, thanks to Luca Neni and my first moments on earth.

This is a bit of public notice, for all those who may think that I am (or am not) what I appear to be.

13
No Toilets for Tesla

I have recently seen *Tesla's Letters*, a play by Jeffrey Stanley, performed by the Timeline Theatre Company in Chicago. It was time well spent. Much of the action takes place at the Tesla Museum in Belgrade, which I visited many years ago as a high school student. I recall it as a rather dark, cold, imposing building, built in the early twentieth century.

The play portrays the complexity of the Balkans and of the recent civil war in the former Yugoslavia. The essential plot is that a PhD student from the United States, Daisy, visits the museum in pursuit of some of Tesla's letters. Things happen, and she learns more about "everything" than she could have ever bargained for.

One of the characters in the play is Biljana, the Communist-era, no-nonsense, uptight, brief, and brisk museum attendant. Her character prompted me to remember a brief story of my wife's visit to the museum.

About ten years ago, Lisa accompanied my mother, Branka, to see the sights of the museum dedicated to Tesla. They happily examined the exhibits and admired both the Serbian genius and the hardworking but quite odd New Yorker that Nikola Tesla eventually became.

After some time, they politely asked the attendant for directions to the toilet. To this, the woman in charge of supervising visitors and providing expert consultation on history, physics, and electricity responded, "I am sorry, but there are no toilets in this building."

An argument ensued. The woman would not admit that there were any toilets in the building and consequently could not point to one!

My wife was stunned by the absurdity of the situation (no toilets in a major museum building!), but my mother took charge. Said she, to the attendant, toe to toe, face-to-face, "My young lady, before World War II, this building was the Italian Embassy. I used to come here for dances that were organized on a regular basis. I can tell you exactly where all the toilets are!"

And she grabbed my wife's hand and pulled her up the marble stairway without hesitation. The woman tried to stop them in vain. A few minutes later, imperiously, the two walked down, hand in hand.

All this seems like an odd triviality, and I have hardly a clue of why I am making a record of it. Perhaps it is because at the core of it, there may lie one of those strange Balkan principles that no one writes down but everyone understands and public servants sometimes like to apply: "Wherever you think you are going, you have to earn the right of passage, especially if the access to it should be free!" Theatrical as it often is, it is a pretty tough philosophy, if you really have to go!

14
We Are All Equal in My Country

I left Yugoslavia over thirty years ago because I could not play the game any longer.

How can I describe this game? To play the game was to pretend that everything was normal. To play the game was to believe we were free because we could get a passport. To play the game was to believe we were at least as good or better than other nations. We convinced ourselves that we had a reasonable future, even after our Great Leader Tito, following his natural death, moved on to other planes of existence.

We did not work too much and thought this to be normal. We had a very good time, taking vacations on the coast and leaves of absence from work, living on borrowed money and on borrowed time. We pledged allegiance to Socialism, and under the table, we did all kinds of naughty non-Socialist things. All this was well accepted and understood.

In fact, I think each of us was split in half, without realizing it, or perhaps with a tacit, deep understanding how the partition worked. The official side joined the Party and believed we had surpassed the East-West division. The private side claimed that it figured out the whole gambit, was able to see the unbecoming facts, and still managed to have a very good time. Often, switching from one side to the other happened in a second. How can I better describe this subjective partition into two halves? I'd like to put my finger on it because it is at the core of our lives at the time. I think the deception we lived with and the game we played had much to do with our pride, with the need to present ourselves in a better light than the real, in a light in which we appeared as normal, conscious, determined individuals, fully in control of our surroundings. The following brief story illustrates my point.

For many years, my mother worked as a translator at a bank. Because of her good knowledge of several European languages and of international banking terminology, she was often given the task of translating agreements, mainly with French and Italian banks. Once in a while, she would be invited to an evening reception at one of the government buildings or at better hotels in town or sometimes at one of the fine homes in Dedinje.

I should note that she hated Communists, mainly because they were "primitive" and had committed injustices against her parents and brothers, and therefore, she was not a member of the ruling party (this misfortune runs in the family). Needless to say, her career was not much to brag about, except that her skills were recognized and utilized, as convenient. Thus, she received occasional invitations to the aforementioned banking soirees, during which I believe she was expected to and did translate deals and pleasantries from one language into another.

Returning from one such soiree in Dedinje, she was given a ride home, in an official limousine, with a French representative of the Société Générale. The driver's decision to drop her off first was prompted by geography—putting a bit of curvature to straight lines, we lived, roughly, between Dedinje and downtown. When the car made the stop in front of our apartment building, at the Boulevard of the Red Army, and my mother thanked the driver and her companion, the Frenchman realized what was going on and made a fuss. Why had he not been dropped off first? After all, he was a representative of the Société Générale and deserved first-class treatment!

According to my mother, she turned to him and said, "In my country, monsieur, simple employees like myself are treated the same as fine people like yourself!" And then she slammed the door and walked away.

I was not present at this exchange and cannot vouch that it took place as described. But that is not important. The important thing is that my mother told me this story with considerable pride. She showed that Frenchmen.

In order to get even with him, she managed to forget much of what her life was about—standing straight before the Communists in power and telling them without words: I am worthy, but I am not one of you.

"So what?" she would say. "He deserved to be dressed down!" But this is my point: here are the two human halves that play the game and do not even see each other.

As absurd as it may sound, simply put, this is why I left.

15
Once I Was Something, but Now I Am Nothing

A few years ago, while strolling down the main drag in Belgrade, walking away from Kalemegdan Park and Terazije and almost to Slavija Square, just near Cvetni Trg (the Square of Flowers), I made the brief acquaintance of a woman. The whole thing lasted about three seconds, during which time the following happened.

She was begging for money, and I made a half circle to avoid her. We understood each other perfectly. I did not change the pace of my walk, and she did not try to intercept me. But we looked at each other, and I saw that this woman, possibly in her forties but looking older, had been beautiful once. In fact, we "connected" for a second: the man in me saw the woman in her—present looks and physique (for I am not what I used to be either) being irrelevant.

She smiled at me, and the begging business was off for a second.

"Once I was something," she said to me as I was passing by, "but now I am nothing." And I was gone. But the message was clear and well understood. And it stayed with me. She was something somewhere, once, and now she is not—displaced from a province at war, sleeping who knows where and who knows with whom. And she knew well enough I was not to be pursued, as one of her former, possibly, class or kin.

Obviously, this brief encounter stayed with me. Having great thoughts at the moment, I put this together with the fall of the Berlin Wall. Before the fall, the country called Yugoslavia was "something"—a bridge between East and West, a place of its own, a place with some strategic, social, and cultural importance. But now (that is, after the fall of the Berlin Wall), its parts and the imaginary whole are "nothing"—bits and pieces of some ancient ethnic puzzle to be given a handout, avoided, or just used by the Main Street of the World, or to be walked by, as is convenient.

It seems the importance of this wall-fall, and more generally of the end of the Cold War, was not properly understood at the time that it happened and shortly thereafter, by at least some of the "auberge Balkanian" participants. In fact, it probably could not have been otherwise; for who wants to admit—unless it is obvious, and even then it is difficult to admit—that one is "nothing"?

But now it is obvious, as it was this past summer, to me, while vacationing in Croatia (who "won the war" supposedly) that all hope (in their case of being an automatic part of the Western world) has come to naught. And Serbs have just failed for the third time in a row to come out in sufficient numbers to vote and elect a president. Being at the moment without a functioning parliament and arguing over the flag colors and national anthem with the Montenegrins, they might as well close the shop and put a big sign on the door saying, "Nothing." I envision, as well, graffiti below saying, "Samuel Beckett was here @#$%&^%."

And truth be told, sometimes, I too feel that once upon a time, I was something but that now I am nothing, especially on a rainy and windy day of a balmy November in Chicago.

I think it was yesterday, or the day before, it is hard to tell, as all days begin to look alike. I do think it was I, but it could have been someone else. I have no way of knowing.

16
A Balkan Koan: Whose Blood Is This?

Koan (in Japanese) is a verbal puzzle, often entirely absurd to common sense, given to trainees in Zen Buddhist monasteries. Perhaps the most famous koan is "What is the sound of one hand clapping?" One is expected to work on such a puzzle, sometimes for years, until it is mentally "resolved." This, at least in principle, leads to a deeper spiritual understanding and inner maturation of the trainee. A classic reference is: An Introduction to Zen Buddhism (with foreword by C.G. Jung) *by D. T. Suzuki (New York: Grove Press, 1964).*

I recently went back to my hometown, for my regular biannual visit. Things have changed over these twenty-five-plus years, but basically, I still follow the same routine. I stay with my mother and sleep in my old bed that long ago became a bit on the short size for my present fifty-some-year-old-body. I visit with relatives and friends. Sometimes I go with my wife, sometimes alone, but the pattern is similar: people, conversation, politics, beat of the city, old hangouts.

My wife tells me that I go back "to gather some of that bittersweet juice," and I think the assessment is correct. Bitter it is, as not much good seems to have happened there since I left; sweet it is, for it used to be home. Many of my friends and neighbors are still where they used to be, and we greet each other in the old familiar way: "*Gde si bre?*" (Where have you been?) and "*komsija*" (neighbor). I am grateful for this as much as I sometimes resent it: I still have a point of reference for my life's travails, but on the other hand, I have to face my own and others' aging, decline, and mortality.

One of my favorite activities is to simply stand in front of our apartment building in the evening and shoot the breeze with the usual crowd that gathers after dinner: a couple of dog owners, a few retirees, neighbors coming home late from work. This gives me a sense of being one of them, although we all know that I am not. Usually after a few teasing comments about "life in America" or regarding "my influence on the NATO policies," things settle down to the usual local chitchat, which I tremendously enjoy.

During one such relaxed evening, as we were discussing the pros and cons of cable Internet, a small dog with big ears, by the name of Mila (Darling) belonging to my retired neighbor Aleksa, marked her usual territory, and another neighbor, Zoran, a man in his fifties, joined us.

Now it is well known that Zoran has a soft spot for stray animals, dogs and cats alike, many of which can be seen roaming the streets of Belgrade.

Zoran has no pets of his own, but he has come into the habit of feeding several cats that come daily to visit below his first-floor apartment kitchen window. In addition, as I found out later, he had been feeding a stray dog by the name of Azra, who had come to recognize him as her master and would come running to greet him as soon as he whistled in a certain special way. Now Azra was a large dog, and my mother and others in the neighborhood had been known to feed her as well. However, officially, Azra was considered, if anyone's, to be Zoran's dog.

As I greeted Zoran, Azra promptly showed up, wanting his attention. The problem was the little dog, Mila, was checking out Zoran's and my shoes at the moment. The territorial issues arose in a split second, and before we had time to look down, the two dogs got into a bitter fight. Having an obvious disadvantage in size and having rather large ears, Mila was quickly treated to a rather unpleasant street-style dogfight and emerged with a bloody ear, screaming to the heavens.

The two animals were promptly separated. Aleksa took Mila aside, and just as we thought the melee was over, he returned, completely beside himself, red in the face, shouting at Zoran. It took me a while to understand what he was saying. He was holding his hand, with a faint trace of blood on it, right in Zoran's face, shouting, "*Cija je ovo krv? Cija je ovo krv?*" ("Whose blood is this? Whose blood is this?")

Now Zoran had been "around the block a few times," meaning he was no stranger to conflict. A rather large man, he had served in the military long ago and had participated in many a Belgrade street demonstration against the Milosevic regime in the 1990s, more than a few of which, as everyone knows, ended with blood on the streets. So Zoran just calmly stood there, making sure his hands were down and tried to bring to reason the furious dog owner. This did not help. Aleksa just could not stop shouting, "Whose blood is this?"

Finally, I slowly stepped in and asked Zoran to take a walk with me to the next corner. And he did. When we returned, everyone had left the scene.

We bid each other a good night, and as I took my long evening walk, I knew that I had a new koan, a "Balkan koan," as I may decide to call it, on my hands: "Whose blood is this?" Seems like a good question indeed. It may take more than three grown men or a couple of years of solitude to find the answer.

17
The Origins of Slavish

A few years ago, my wife and I traveled east. Leaving Chicago, we took Route 90 and drove straight to Erie, Pennsylvania. We stopped at a brand-new eight-unit motel. Being the only guests, we picked a room close to the fields and a muddy construction site. "This is as close as we'll get to camping" was my comment.

We soon settled into two rather comfortable white plastic chairs in front of our motel room door with a bottle of wine and some cheese and salami. It was already dark; we just watched the lights of traffic passing at some distance, and it was fine with us. Not long thereafter, a big Cadillac pulled in, and a tall, well-built man in his sixties stepped out. "Howdy, folks," he said. "I am the owner of this motel. Just came by to see if everything's all right." It sure was.

We chatted for a while, and he confided in us that his wife of many years had passed away five years ago and that he built the motel "just to have something to do." This was fine with us too. We said we were sorry about his loss. "I got over it," he said. "You gotta move on. Got a Laundromat down the road too."

After a while, he turned to me. "Where you from, big fella? You got a funny accent."

"Eastern Europe," I said.

"Slovakia?" he inquired.

"Yep," I said, not quite knowing why.

"I have Slavish blood too," he said.

"Really?" I feigned a bit of surprise and interest.

"Yes," he said. "My grandmother only spoke Slavish to us kids at home. I don't remember a word, but that's what she spoke to us."

"Wow," my wife said as we looked at each other. "Some language, Slavish."

"They were very poor over there, before they came here," he said, as if apologizing. "And they suffered in all kinds of wars too. And you, big fella, you speak Slavish?" he asked me.

"Not really," I said. "Too many cases, genders, grammar, and stuff."

"I know it," he said. "Everything's complicated over there."

A pleasant, simple silence fell upon us. "Well," he said after a while, "gotta go pick up my girlfriend and have something to eat down the road. She's from around here," he added, "used to work in my motel."

"Well," I said, "are you sure it was Slovakia?"

"Not really," he said, "something Slavish, but it was a long time ago. Not quite sure."

"Okay," I said.

My wife and I sat there for a while longer, watching cars go by. First of all, the "Slavish" language does not exist. Neither does a country by the name of, I suppose, Slavia.

As the wine got deeper into my cells and into my soul, I began to see through to the possible origins of this nonexistent language. It possibly came from many an immigrant grandmother who spoke of things (of horrors) of the past that no sane child would want to understand. And the child then, conveniently, perceived it as a murmur, an embarrassing remembrance of some faraway past that bears no importance on the present. For an immigrant's child's present (I venture to opine) is perpetually turned toward a more or less promising future, and the grandmother's role is gradually reduced to the one of producer of *kolacki, strudel, burek,* or *pita.* And the murmured language loaded with stories of pogroms and poverty is forgotten and even its name is forgotten or conveniently mispronounced.

I must say that I was rather happy with this somewhat simple theory. It fit well the temporary surroundings of our motel and the brief encounter with a man whose face we knew we would never see again.

After a while, my wife said, "I think he recognized you though, as his Slavish brother."

"Of course," I said smartly, "his grandfather fought mine in World War I. They probably played a game of cards or two on no-man's-land, during a break, while their cannons slept."

She said nothing, and my eloquence was exhausted for good. In the distance, the endless line of car headlights kept rolling by, until we quietly drank the last of the wine and called it a night.

18
The Phone Call

The first thing that comes to mind, after all the processions and formalities have been performed and I have returned to normal life, is this: I have no one to call on a Sunday morning. Or, I have no one to call on most mornings, as I have, in the last few years, come into a habit of calling my mother almost every day. She had been failing slowly but consistently, losing some memory and things like her glasses, becoming unable to walk to the bus or the neighborhood store.

Being an only child, one of my fears of adult life has been that phone call, early in the morning, as I envisioned it. And it did come one Tuesday morning in late January, as I was stretching out, making coffee, and checking e-mail. There were several "urgent" messages across the information spectrum, including my mobile phone. My wife kept her calm and let me take my time to face the facts.

The week before, I had just returned from spending ten days with my mother in the apartment I grew up in and the one she had lived in for the past fifty years, on South Boulevard in Belgrade. The last evening of my stay we spent in a jovial mood; we had a bit to drink and talked almost till midnight. She was a bit funny, or loopy, or nutty, as you wish. We drank the liquor called Gorki List ("the bitter leaf," a Serb production), which was a bit odd for her to indulge in, as she had been a consistent fan of Bailey's Irish Cream.

We had two or three glasses, and after each, she would get up and begin to "go to bed," but then she would return and sit back down in the armchair facing me. She limped a bit, repeating that "it was nothing at all."

So there she sat, telling me repeatedly, unexplainably, "*Kako god vi kazes, gospodin*" (Whatever you say, sir), but with the polite "*vi*" ("you") form mixed with the informal "*kazes*" (say) form, and "*gospodin*" (sir) used in the wrong declension imitating what in Serbia is known perhaps as "an uneducated person addressing a higher-up, trying to show sophistication." She was in a good mood. "Did I ever tell you how I met Stalin?" she once asked.

"I think you did," I said.

We then had another round.

I knew her end was in sight, but I expected it would take a year for things to really go bad. My flight was to take off at 6:00 a.m. the next morning, and I got up at 3:15. I left the apartment at 4:00 a.m., cab waiting, and I did not peek into her room. I could hear her breathing, as she was sound asleep. A part of me was afraid she would die right there and then, and I would have to reschedule my flights and work obligations. So I just walked out and hopped into the cab, continuing my prior conversation with the driver. In Belgrade, if you can, you get "your own cabbie". Mine was always two minutes early on the dot, and he had good stories to tell.

Nine days later, on a Tuesday morning, I made my coffee, did my exercises, took a shower, and then, with my wife quietly waiting for me to get to business, began to pick up messages. Thanks to my wife's prowess with the Internet and ticket booking, at 5:00 p.m., I was sitting on a plane going back to Belgrade, apartment keys in hand, the apartment ownership papers in my folder, black tie and black jacket in my carry-on luggage.

A week later, I was back at home, back at work. "How does it feel?" asked my wife, looking at me with sympathy.

"Oh, fine," I said. "I just want to make that call, and there is no one there to pick it up."

GLOSSARY[2]

ajvar. You grill red peppers; let them cool off; peel off the skin; grind them with oil, garlic, and many secret ingredients; place the resultant production in a jar; and save for the winter. It always works.

Beria. Lavrentiy Pavlovich Beria (1899–1953), the longest-lived and most influential of Stalin's secret police chiefs. He did not make many friends on the way up. He was put on trial and shot in the back of the head in short order by a general of the Soviet military once everyone in the Politburo agreed.

comrade. In Serbian, *drug,* masculine, and *drugarica,* feminine, the official way to address a person after the revolution in Yugoslavia and elsewhere; "Madame" and "Sir" (*gospodja* and *gospodin*) had to be dropped as remnants of the "language of the exploiting classes."

deda. Grandfather in Serbian.

---

[2] Note: Specific information is based on that in Wikipedia.org.

gymnasium. A serious kind of high school, prevalent in Germanic and some East European countries. Philosophy, Mathematics, Physics, Latin and Old Greek were taught and "gymnastics" (physical education) was often compulsory. It prepared one for college, but if one did not go to college, one was entirely unprepared for life after graduating.

Kočevski Rog. According to the Wikipedia article, "it was a location where thousands of people, such as the Slovene Home Guard and their families, were executed by special units of the Yugoslav Army in late May 1945. They were thrown into various pits and caves, which were then sealed with explosives. Several thousand (between 10,000 and 12,000, according to certain sources) war prisoners, repatriated by the British military authorities from Austria, where they had fled, died in these post-war summary executions." (http://en.wikipedia.org/wiki/Kocevski_Rog, August 12, 2011.) Among those executed were, it seems, at least 3,000 members of the Serbian Volunteer Corps.

Milosevic. Slobodan Milosevic (1941–2006), ruler of Yugoslavia (1997–2000) and of Serbia (1989–1997). My mother worked as a French translator under him in *Beobanka* in Belgrade in the late 1970s before he went into politics. She told me he was a good banking manager. I think she voted for him at least on one occasion, when he was running for one or another presidential position. The rest is the unpleasant and complex history of the disintegration of a country, of the civil war, of NATO bombing, of political assassinations etc. "Fifteen years of my life that was wasted" - someone commented on this period.

Molotov. Vyacheslav Mikhailovich Molotov (1890–1986), a Soviet politician and diplomat, a leading figure in the Soviet government from the 1920s to 1957. The expression "Molotov cocktail" was apparently coined by the Finns who threw them at "Molotov's tanks," which were allegedly "bringing them food" across the border.

pindjur. Similar to Ajvar, but the esoteric secrets of its "perpetual becoming" were not passed on to me at my graduation from childhood innocence. It's something like *ratatouille* in France or *capponata* in Italy. So many secret recipes and so little time!

Proust. Marcel Proust (1871–1922) French novelist, critic, and essayist best known for his monumental *À la recherche du temps perdu (In Search of Lost Time,* earlier translated as *Remembrance of Things Past).* It was published in seven parts between 1913 and 1927.

Société Générale. A big French bank (1864–present). Once I almost opened an account with this bank, just in homage to my mother. But it was getting late, and I had to take the Metro across town. Now that

Francs are history and English is the lingua franca, I doubt I will try it again. One never knows though.

Stalin. Joseph Vissarionovich Stalin (1878–1953), ruler of the Soviet Union between 1924 and 1953. They say that his speech after Lenin's death lasted seven hours. Everything about Stalin is pretty serious and pretty grim.

Tesla. Nikola Tesla (1856–1943), he invented electricity as it runs through our households today. Tesla was a genius and an odd fellow. He dined at Waldorf Astoria Hotel in New York City wearing white gloves as form of germ protection. I've also read that he wrote poems for a dove that visited him at his hotel window. His life and accomplishments are historical, especially if you are of Serbian heritage or if you study electrical engineering.

Tito. Josip Broz Tito (1892–1980), ruler of Yugoslavia from 1945 to 1980. He was the "good king" of post-World War II Yugoslavia, and in later years, he liked white uniforms and big cigars. He kept Yugoslavia out of Soviet dominance and played a fine game between the East and the West. All children loved him. I loved him too when I was a child.

Family Photos

My grandfather Stevan, leaning on his saber, standing, fourth from your right, 1915.

My grandparents, Branka and her brothers, with their grandmother Zivkovic, in 1927 or 1928.

My parents, in 1951 or 1952.

Branka, at work, probably at the Federal Bank of Yugoslavia, in 1960's.

Aunt Lala, at the "old house", circa 1990.

Our apartment building, on South Boulevard, Belgrade, 1998.

Branka, in her apartment, Belgrade, 2005.

Branka's room with a view, 2005.

Lisa on Lake Shore Drive, Chicago, 2010.

90

About the Author

Borko Jovanovic was born in Vrsac and grew up in Belgrade, Serbia, where he spent the first half of his life. He moved to the United States in 1980 to study Mathematics. Presently he works as a scientist and lives in Chicago with his wife. He writes and has published poetry, short stories and plays in Serbian and in English.